A Working Musician's Joke Book

Sound And Vision

A Working Musician's Joke Book

Daniel G. Theaker

Illustrations
Mike Freen

Sound And Vision
Toronto

Table Of Contents

Author's Note & Acknowledgements

This collection of music jokes is the culmination of a few years of really intense joking among my friends and collegues in the music industry. The most common place one hears music jokes is either during rehearsal or at a gig ('at a gig' can also mean, at the pub after the show while consuming a concoction of murky brown liquid in very large quantities'). From performers, arrangers, composers, publishers, teachers and students, many people have contributed to, and helped me compile this book.

The first person to get my thanks is Mike Freen for his excellent drawings in my book. My personal editing department gets thanks as well. Keith McGuire, Jennifer Kendall and Susan Freen (Mike's Mom) all read the manuscript and had to put up with really bad jokes and re-read the ones that they had already heard a thousand times or more. Thanks go to Steven and John Loweth at Mayfair Music in Toronto for believing in my original musical compositions and for introducing me to Geoff Savage. Mr. Savage of Sound And Vision gets to take a bow for supporting my work and for being patient while I explained the merits of this type of book.

Finally I would like to thank Captain Terry Porter and the musicians of the Regimental Band Of The Governor General's Foot Guards in Ottawa for listening to my jokes and giving me a fun place to play the flute. Happy joking.

Daniel G. Theaker, B.Mus.

Introduction

Many people have different impressions of the lives of the average everyday professional musician. This book should shed some light on what really goes on. From the classical artist to the pop star, everyone gets picked on.

Some of the humour presented here may need some explaination from the people who actually play the instruments in question. I've taken out the *really* dirty jokes so those of you that are faint of heart need not be worried about an oncoming embolism or heart attack.

I hope you enjoy the *Working Musician's Joke Book.*

Daniel G. Theaker, B. Mus.

Preface

There is no record of the very first musical joke ever told, but it probably had something to do with a couple of cavemen (excuse me, cave*people*), a large rock and some sort of woolly mammoth bone.

But the very second musical joke ever told, we now know with reasonable certainty, was considered hilariously funny at the time and even today can still raise a chuckle. (At least among those of us relatively fluent in early Cenozoic forms of communication. If you aren't, there's not much point reproducing it here, and there isn't really time to give you a crash course.) Anyway, suffice it to say it involved a loincloth, a large club and some *other* sort of woolly mammoth bone. In fact, some paleo-humorologists believe it may be a variation of that first woolly mammoth joke, just as today there are so many jokes about lightbulbs or lawyers. (Example: Why are mammoths so woolly? Because Thinsulate hadn't been invented yet. *Ba-dum-bum.*)

Since then, musical jokes have flourished along with the art form (or, in the case of rock music, they've flourished anyway). Haydn was a great joker, and Mozart was likely to grab your wig and toss it around the room. Beethoven liked a good laugh, especially if it was at someone else's expense (although a Romantic composer, Beethoven was always broke). Stravinsky's humor tended to be subtle and mischievous, while in the case of John Cage, you could argue that everything's funny—but the joke's on us.

From his firsthand experience as a working musician (meaning he has a fair amount of spare time on his hands), Daniel Theaker has gathered together in this little book a motley collection of musical jokes—some old, some new, some borrowed and (mindful of a PG rating) only a few of them blue. Whatever instrument you play or part you sing, there's bound to be some here that apply to you— or rather, that you can tell about some other instrument or voice part. They're mostly interchangeable anyway. If there's a tuba player you want to make fun of, just take one of the trombone jokes and tell it down the octave. (For violists, just tell one of the violin jokes v-e-e-r-r-r-y s-l-o-w-l-y.)

So have fun, and try not to burst out laughing during a performance. You might wake someone up.

David W. Barber

The Keyboard

Among keyboards, there are three main instruments: the piano, the harpsichord, and the organ. Among these, the piano and the organ receive the most attention.

The piano is probably the single most important percussion instrument around. (You didn't realize it was a drum did you?) It is frequently used in solo recital or chamber music and is essential for rehearsal purposes. Most pianists loathe having to accompany other instruments, (violins, flutes, etc.) unless they are being paid. When they do get paid, however, they merely tolerate the ordeal. I mean, the pianist thinks to him or herself, "THEY only have to learn ONE line on the staff, whereas WE have to learn up to FOUR lines, assorted chords and other unpleasant oddities."

The keyboard player's lot in life is a lonely one, so for their sake, have a little patience, please.

Piano

The audience at a piano recital were appalled when a telephone rang just off stage. Without missing a beat, the soloist glanced in the direction of the stage manager and said, "If that's my agent, tell him I'm working."

Why is an 11-foot concert grand better than a studio upright?

— *Because it makes a bigger kaboom when dropped over a cliff.*

What key do you get when you drop a piano down a mine shaft?

— *A-flat minor.*

What do you use to tie a piano to a moving van so the piano won't fall over?

— *Root position chords.*

"Where have I seen you before, young man?" a judge demanded, looking down at the defendant. "I gave your daughter piano lessons last year, Your Honour." "Ah yes, I remember you now," recalled the judge. "Guilty. 25 years!"

For whom did the inventor design a piano with stationary keys?

— *For people who would rather play the violin.*

For whom did the inventor design a silent piano?

— *For people who don't like music.*

Why was the piano invented?
— *So the singer would have a place to put her beer.*

Why are pianists' fingers like lightning?
— *They rarely strike the same place twice.*

Up at 'Pearly Gates Customs', St. Peter was checking people through. "Occupation?" he asked the first person. "Physician," came the reply. "Good. In you go." When asked the same question, the next person replied, "Kindergarten teacher." Same response. "Right. In you go." When the pianist turn came he said, "Piano player." "Oh good, you're here! Go around the side and up the stairs. You can change in the washroom in the hallway."

Organ

Why did J. S. Bach have 20 children?
— *His organ didn't have any stops.*

What's better than roses on your piano?
— *Tulips on your organ.*

What is worse than a dead skunk on your piano?
— *An infected beaver on your organ.*

15

Why doesn't heaven have a pipe organ?
— *Because they needed the keys in hell to make accordians.*

Why are organists similar to a broken-winded carriage horse?
— *They are always longing for another stop.*

How many organists does it take to change a lightbulb?
— *Two. One to change the bulb and one to complain that the switch doesn't have any combination pistons.*

The organist was having his annual 'Whoop-it-up-once-a-year' party with the other church organists, when he came across a musician's-only club. He had heard rumours about this exclusive club and thought that they should check it out. They entered and after a thorough security check (Musician's Union), were told of the club's unique format. "In this club, our guests have the choice of parties they may wish to attend. Each door has a number on the front corresponding to the intelligence quotient of the participants inside." They were all suitably impressed. "Maybe this time we might finally meet some people we can talk to." they mused. The first door that they came across said room 150. Inside, they found Phillip Glass, Harry Somers and R. Murray Schafer having a lively debate on whether John Cage had some good ideas or not. "Too stuffy." they thought. The next room was room 100. Inside they found brass quintets, woodwind quintets and people of their own instrument species generally having a happy time. "Nice," they thought, "but not our kind of people." Finally, they came to room 50. Inside, they found two long-haired guys in leather sitting on regular bar stools. "Who are you?" asked the organist. "We're drummers, man. We were told to make you feel welcome."

Synthesizer

How can you tell if there is a synth player at your door?
— *You hear knocking, but you can't tell if it's real or not.*

The Orchestra

The orchestra is made up of many different types of instruments. It goes without saying that it takes a certain type of personality to play these unwieldly contraptions. Not everyone, for instance, is suited to play a violin. Others, it would seem, are better suited to play the French horn.

This section is divided into five parts: woodwind, brass, strings, percussion and those pesky individuals who all their lives wanted desperately to play baseball, the conductor.

The humour in this section is in score order. For those of you who are orchestrally impaired, the order is as a conductor would read an musical score. Try to follow along as best you can.

We didn't know where to put that bizarre contraption called the saxophone so we lumped it in with the woodwinds. As well, those baritone-hating euphonium players are seen here loitering behind the trombones. Where do they get these instruments?

Woodwinds

Flute & Piccolo

How many flute players does it take to screw in a lightbulb?

— *Just one, but she will twist the bulb back and forth for half an hour before she gets it right.*

18

What key is the alto flute pitched in?
— *G(ee), I don't know either.*

How do flute players greet each other?
— *Hi, I played that piece in junior high.*

What is the definition of a minor second?
— *Two flutes playing in unison.*

How do you get two piccolos to play in tune?
— *Shoot one of them.*

What is the quickest and easist way to manufacture diamonds?
— *Have a flute player sit on a bag of coal.*

How do you know when a flutist is at your door?
— *The doorbell speeds up.*

What do you call a flutist without a significant other?
— *Homeless.*

How many flute players does it take to change a lightbulb?
— *One, but he will spend $3,000 on a handcrafted, sterling-silver bulb.*

Where do we wish bad flute players would play?
— *In a galaxy far, far away.*

How are flutists like linoleum?
— *Lay them well the first time and you can walk on them forever.*

Two woodwind players were walking down the street. One of them said to the other, "Who was that flute I saw you with last night?" The other responded, "That was no flute, that was my fife."

How many flute players does it take to change a lightbulb?

— *Only one, but she'll break 10 bulbs before she realizes they can't be pushed in.*

How do concert band flute players change a lightbulb?

— *They ask their boyfriends to do it for them.*

Oboe

How do you get five oboes to play in tune?

— *Shoot four of them.*

What is the definition of a major second?

— *Two Baroque oboes playing in tune.*

What are flaming oboes good for?

— *Setting bassoons on fire.*

How do you get an oboe player to play A-flat?

— *Take the batteries out of her tuner.*

What is perfect pitch?

— *When you lob an oboeist into a dumpster without hitting the rim*

How many oboeists does it take to change a lightbulb?

— *Only one, but by the time she finishes shaving the tip you will need a new one.*

Why would anybody want to be on the last chair in the flute section?

— *To keep the oboe player company*

English Horn

Why is playing an English horn solo like wetting your pants?

— *Both give you a warm feeling but no one cares.*

What is an English horn teacher called?
— *A Tudor tooter tutor.*

How many English horn players does it take to change a lightbulb?
— *One, but he will fall off the ladder from gyrating too much.*

How do you tune two oboes?
— *Shoot both of them.*

Clarinet

Why do clarinet players leave their cases on the dashboard?
— *So they can park in the handicap zones.*

How many clarinetists does it take to change a lightbulb?
— *Only one, but it takes him forever to find just the right bulb.*

What is the difference between the sound of a clarinet and a cat in heat?
— *Nothing if the cat is healthy.*

What is the difference between a clarinet and an onion?
— *No one cries when you chop up a clarinet.*

Alto Clarinet

What is the definition of a nerd?
— *Someone who owns their own alto clarinet.*

Where do alto clarinet players play best?
— *In traffic.*

Bass Clarinet

What do you call a bass clarinetist with half a brain?
— *Musically gifted.*

What's the purpose of the bell on a bass clarinet?
— *Storing the ashes from the rest of the instrument.*

How do you keep someone from jumping up and down on a bass clarinet?
— *Why would you want them to stop?*

Saxophone

Alto Sax

As a guy walks through a forest, a fairy suddenly appears and offers him a free wish, whatever it might be. So he takes out a pocket atlas and points towards different continents: "See, here, is suffering, there, is hunger and over there, people are tortured. I want all people to be free and healthy! Can you do that?" The fairy sighs and says: "Well, this is very hard, even for me. Is there a chance that you can come up with another wish instead that would make it a little easier?" The guy answers: "As a matter of fact, there is. See, I play the soprano saxophone, and I have such a hard time with the intonation in the upper register. Do you think you could ....?" "Okay, okay, let's look at your atlas one more time ..."

What is the difference between a saxophone and a chainsaw?
— *It's all in the grip.*

What is the difference between a saxophone and a train whistle?
— *Train whistles have tone quality.*

What is the difference between four saxes and four lawnmowers?
— *Absolutely nothing.*

How many C melody sax players can you fit into a phone booth?

— *All of them.*

What do a saxophone and a baseball have in common?

— *People cheer when you hit them with a bat.*

Why did the saxophone player play lots of wrong notes?

— *He thought the key signature was just a suggestion.*

How many alto sax players does it take to change a light bulb?

— *Three. One to change the bulb and two to debate how David Sanborn would have done it.*

What is the difference between an alto sax and a lawnmower?

— *You can tune a lawnmower.*

What is another difference between an alto sax and a lawnmower?

— *Vibrato.*

Tenor & Baritone Sax

If you were lost in the forest, who would you trust for directions, an in-tune tenor sax player, an out-of-tune tenor sax player, or the Easter Bunny?
— *The out-of-tune tenor sax player. (The other two don't exist.)*

How do you put down a tenor saxophone?
— *Confuse it with a bass clarinet.*

What's the difference between the creationist theory of the origin of life and a tenor sax?
— *The theory dosn't have as many leaks.*

What is the difference between a baritone saxophone and a chainsaw?
— *The exhaust.*

How do you make a baritone saxophone sound like a chainsaw?
— *Add vibrato.*

Bassoon

How do you insult a saxophone player?
— *Call him a bassoonist.*

What is the difference between a bassoon and a trampoline?

— *You take your shoes off to jump on a trampoline.*

Why did the chicken cross the road?

— *To get away from the bassoon recital.*

What is the difference between a bassoon and a mud puddle?

— *You take your shoes off to jump on a mud puddle.*

Brass & Percussion

Trumpet

What do trumpet players use for birth control?
— *Their personalities.*

What are trumpets made from?
— *Leftover saxophone parts.*

Why do trumpet players only use one hand to play their horn?
— *Because the other one is too busy.*

Why do you bury trumpet players six feet under?
— *Because deep down they really are nice people.*

How many trumpet players does it take to change a lightbulb?
— *Five. One to change it and four to say how much better they would have done it.*

What is the difference between a lawnmower and a trumpet?
— *The neighbour gets mad if you don't return the lawnmower.*

How do trumpet players greet each other?
— *Hi, I'm better than you.*

How many trumpet players does it take to change a lightbulb?
— *Five. One to change the bulb and four to contemplate how Louis Armstrong would have done it.*

What is the difference between a trumpet player and a horse's backside?
— *I don't know either.*

How do you know when a trumpet player is at your front door?
— *The doorbell shrieks.*

What is the difference between a trumpet player and a savings bond?

— *The savings bond matures and earns money.*

Solve the following equation:

Person 'A' was walking down the street with person 'B'. Person 'A' says, "What's 10% of nothing?". Match the trumpet player and his agent with Person 'A' and Person 'B'.

At one of the many summer festivals in the area, a friend of mine was playing the usual trumpet solo for the big band that he founded with the band leader. The newest member of the ensemble was a flashy young trumpet player who was hired to fill in for this particular gig. When the solo part came up on the chart, the patriarch of the band (my friend) was getting ready to play when all of a sudden the young new guy leapt up and just wailed out a beautiful trumpet solo. My friend was upset at the young man's actions and scolded him for them. "I've been playing that solo for 30 years," he said, "and no one has EVER upstaged me during that time!" The young man did not understand his elder's anguish, "Hey, sorry, man," he replied, "I was just doing what the chart said, man. See, it says right here 'Take It!', you know, T... A ... C ... E... T!"

Two guys are standing on the side of the road. One's a trumpet player and the other one doesn't have any money either.

French Horn

The wife of a prominent French horn player arrived at her lawyer's office requesting a divorce from her husband. "What are the grounds?" asked the lawyer. "Cruel and unusual punishment," she said. "Could you describe for me what it is exactly that he has done to you?" he asked "Well, my husband is a French horn player in the orchestra. The problem is that every time he kisses me, he thinks that I'm a French horn and tries to stick his hand up my butt!"

How many French horn players does it take to change a lightbulb?
— *Just one, but he'll spend two hours checking the bulb for alignment and leaks.*

How do you know when a French horn player is at your door?
— *The doorbell drags.*

How do you get the viola section to sound like the horn section?
— *Have them miss every other note.*

How do French horn players traditionally greet each other?
— *Hi, I played that piece last year.*

What is the difference between a French horn player and a seamstress?

— *The seamstress is often heard saying "Tuck the frills."*

What did the French horn player say after the conductor yelled "Back to bar one!"?

— *Where are we? My parts aren't numbered.*

How many good French horn players does it take to screw in a lightbulb?

— *Only one, but good luck trying to find him.*

Why is a French horn a divine instrument?

— *Because man plays it but only God knows what comes out of it.*

How do you make a French horn sound like a trombone?

— *Take your hand out of the bell and lose all sense of taste.*

Said the conductor to his brass section: "Guys, I need you to play with more dynamics!" One of the horn players: "But boss, that's already as loud as we can play!"

Trombone

A country & western singer and a trombone player are found dead on an open road. What is the difference between the two?

— *The singer was probably on his way to a gig.*

How many trombone players does it take to change a lightbulb?

— *Only one but he will spend an hour trying to figure out what position it needs to be in.*

What do four trombones sound like at the bottom of the lake?

— *A good idea.*

What is the difference between a trombone player's kid and the other kids in the park?

— *He can't swing and doesn't know how to use the slide.*

What do you call a trombone player with a beeper?

— *An optimist.*

How does a trombonist interpret 'detaché'?
— *Without slide.*

How do you know if there is a trombone player at your door?
— *The doorbell drags.*

What was the trombone section's most famous entry?
— *Was that it?*

Define a successful trombone player.
— *He owes his success to letting everything slide.*

What is the best kind of trombone?
— *A broken one.*

Why do trombonists get worried when they read the 'Kama Sutra'?
— *Because they only know seven positions.*

How do you prevent a trombone player from drowning?
— *Take your foot off his head.*

How many trombonists does it take to change a lightbulb?
— *One, but he will do it too loudly.*

What is the difference between a trombone and a chainsaw?

— *It's still easier to improvize on a chainsaw.*

What is the definition of a gentleman?

— *Someone who knows how to play a trombone but refrains from doing so.*

What did Captain Picard say when he entered a jazz club and saw a trombonist on stage?

— *"Computer: End program!"*

Someone asks a trombonist: "What's the subdominant of F major?"

— *The trombonist is confused: "What??? I thought F major was the subdominant!"*

How do you make a trombone sound like a French horn?

— *Stick your hand in the bell and play a lot of wrong notes.*

What is the difference between a dead snake and a dead trombonist on the road?

— *There are skid marks in front of the snake.*

Bass Trombone

What is the difference between a bass trombone and a chain saw?
— *Nothing if you hold the chainsaw very still.*

What is the dynamic range of a bass trombone?
— *On or off.*

Euphonium

What is the difference between a euphonium and chainsaw?
— *Vibrato. However, you can minimize this by holding the chainsaw very still.*

How do you know when a euphonium player is at your door?
— *His hat says 'Pizza Hut'.*

Bumper sticker found on a euphonium player's car:
— *"Baritones are for losers!"*

How do you get a euphonium player out of a tree?
— *Cut the noose.*

What do you do if you run over a euphonium?
— *Back up.*

Tuba

What do you clean a sousaphone with?
— *With a 'tuba' toothpaste*

What is the range of a tuba?
— *10 metres if you have a good arm.*

How do you get the viola section to sound like the tuba section?
— *Have them miss every other note.*

How do you know when a tuba player is at your door?
— *The doorbell drags.*

Define 'bar line'.
— *A gathering of tuba players at a popular drinking establishment.*

How does a tuba player fix his tuba?
— *With a tuba glue.*

What does a tuba player call a diminished fifth?
— *An empty bottle of Scotch.*

Two tuba players were walking past a bar and...
— *Oh wait, you've heard that one already haven't you?*

Why do tuba players have pea-sized brains?
— *Because alcohol has swelled them.*

Why can't tuba players hold office jobs?
— *They are low on character, below the staff, and they spend too much time resting.*

Percussion

How do know when a percussionist is at your front door?
— *The knocking gets faster* (see Drums).

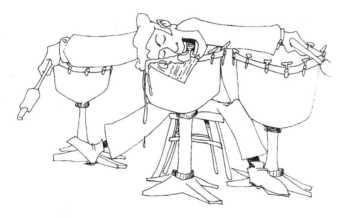

What did the timpani player get on his I. Q. test?
— *Drool.*

What did the xylophone player say at her first gig?
— *Would you like fries with that, sir?*

Why do bands have bass players?
— *To translate for the drummers.*

String Instruments

Violin

A String Quartet is composed of the following :
One good violinist.
One bad violinist.
One really bad violinist who felt more comfort-
able on viola.
One cellist who hates all violinists.

How do you get a violin to play a downbow stac-
cato?
— *Put a tenuto mark over a whole note and mark
it 'Solo.'*

Why does a violinist keep a cloth under his chin
when he plays?
— *Because there aren't any spit valves.*

What is the difference between a violinist and a
dog?
— *The dog knows when to stop scratching.*

A violinist and a violist are standing on a soccer pitch. There is a crisp $100 bill in the middle of the field. Who gets there first?

— *The violist. That violinist isn't going anywhere for only $100.*

What is the definition of a cluster chord?

— *The 2nd violins all playing on a 'C'.*

What is the diffence between the first and last desks in the 2nd violin section?

— *About half a measure.*

What is the difference between a violin and a fiddle?

— *A fiddle is fun to listen to.*

How can you tell if a violin is out of tune?

— *The bow is moving.*

What is the difference between a violin and a fiddle?

— *Nobody minds if you spill beer on a fiddle.*

Why would you not hammer a nail with your violin?

— *You might bend the nail.*

43

What is a brain surgeon from Rome who plays the violin called?

— *A Nero-surgeon.*

A violinist was signing autographs after his debut recital. "There isn't much room here on the program," he said to his young fan, "what should I write?" A colleague overheard this and quipped, "Write your repertoire."

Viola

Why are viola jokes so short?

— *So violinists can understand them.*

How do you get the viola section to play Spiccato?

— *Write a whole note with Solo written above it.*

How do you get your violin to sound like a viola?

— *Play in the low register with a lot of wrong notes.*

How do you get a second violin to sound like a viola?

— *Sit in the back and don't play.*

How many violists does it take to tile a floor?
— *Only one but you have to slice him very thinly.*

What is the range of a viola?
— *As far as you can kick it.*

What is the difference between a washing machine and a violist?
— *Vibrato.*

Bobby came home from school one day and said to his mom, "Mommy, I learned the alphabet today! The rest of the class could only get up to F and I got all the way through!" His mom replied, "That's because you're a violist, Bobby" The next day came and Bobby said, "Mommy, I counted to a hundred in school today. Everybody else could only get to 60." "That's because you're a violist, dear," came the reply. So again, the very next day Johnny came home with,

"Mommy, I'm taller than everyone in my class. Is that because I'm a violist?" "No dear, that's because you're 26."

How do you get a violist to play something 'pianissimo tremolando'?
— *Mark it Solo.*

What do you do with a dead violist?
— *Move him back a desk.*

Why won't violas show up on digital recordings?
— *Digital recordings eliminate all unneccessary noise.*

How do you know if a viola section is at your door?
— *No one knows when to come in.*

What is the difference between violists and terrorists?
— *Terrorists have sympathizers.*

Did you hear about the violist who bragged that she could play 64th notes?
— *The other string players didn't believe her so she played them one.*

How do you keep your violin from getting stolen?

— *Put it in a viola case.*

What do a viola and a court case have in common?

— *Everybody is relieved when the case is closed.*

What is the difference between a violin and a viola?

— *Violas burn longer.*

We all know that a viola is better than a violin because it burns longer. But why does it burn longer?

— *It's usually still in the case.*

What is the difference between a viola and a trampoline?

— *You take your shoes off to jump on a trampoline.*

One afternoon during rehearsal, an oboe player and a viola player were knocking each other about with their fists, severely injuring each other. "What in heaven's name are you two doing?" exclaimed the conductor. After two burly bass players separated them, the oboe player shreiked, "She broke all of my reeds and now I can't play!" The viola player, looking for swift justice, proclaimed, "Oh yeah, well she turned one of my pegs all the way up and I can't tell which one!"

Cello

How do you get a cellist to play fortissimo?
— *Write pp espressivo.*

Why was the cellist angry at the conductor?
— *Because he told her to stop scratching that thing between her legs.*

What is the difference between a cello and a coffin?
— *The coffin has the corpse on the inside.*

How do you make a cello sound beautiful?
— *Sell it and buy a violin.*

Why are orchestra intermissions limited to 20 minutes?
— *So you don't have to retrain the cellists.*

Double-Bass

I met a bass player who was so bad that even his section noticed.

A bass player arrived for rehearsal of Handel's *Messiah* a few minutes late. When the conductor asked him if he wanted a few minutes to tune he replied, "Why? Isn't it the same as last year?"

How many bass players does it take to change a lightbulb?
— *None. Bass players are so macho that they prefer to walk in the dark and stub their toes on the furniture.*

A friend of mine took a vacation to a fairly obscure tropical island. When he got off the boat he heard drumming from every part of the island. Being relatively adventurous, he thought, "I can get into this." The problem was the drumming never stopped. He tried to sleep—drumming. He tried to eat—drumming. He asked one of the local native people to explain this slightly odd phenomenon. The little man explained, "Drums play all day and all night. Very bad if drums stop." My friend was curious and more than a little frightened, "What would happen if the drums stopped?" The little man cautioned, "When drums stop, bass solo begins!"

How many bass players does it take to change a lightbulb?
— *None. The piano player can do it with his left hand.*

Why is a double bass better than a cello?
— *A double bass holds more beer.*

Harp

Why is the harpist the busiest musician in the orchestra?
— *She spends half the time tuning her harp and the other half playing it out of tune!*

What happened to the guy who fell through a harp?

— *He is in the hospital. Rooms 25 to 40.*

What is the definition of a quarter tone?

— *A harpist tuning her unison strings.*

How long does a harp stay in tune?

— *About 30 minutes, or until someone opens a door.*

Why are harps like elderly parents?

— *Both are unforgiving and hard to get out of cars.*

What is worse than a harp ensemble playing Bach transcriptions?

— *I can't think of anything either.*

Conductors

From an orchestral musician's point of view, the road to conducting is paved with venom. As a rule, conductors receive plenty of it. These slimy, slithering reptilian creatures, however, receive more than their fair share of the pie when it comes to the charms of the female singers and instrumental soloists.

As with many other things musical, this is merely convention and not always the rule. It makes one wonder what conductors have that the ordinary Joe musician lacks. Perhaps there is a reason why there are so few good conductors.

What fun would it be if everybody knew their secrets?

Why are conductors' hearts coveted for transplant?
— *They've had so little use.*

How many conductors does it take to change a lightbulb?
— *One, but, then again who's really watching?*

Why did they bury the conductor 20 feet in the earth?
— *Because deep down—DEEP DOWN—he was really a nice guy.*

What's the difference between a band director and a bag of fertilizer?
— *The bag.*

How many conductors does it take to change a lightbulb?
— *Only one, but I wouldn't expect YOU to understand.*

What is the difference between a bull and an orchestra?
— *The bull has the horns in the front and the ass in the back.*

How much does the average conductor weigh?
— *28 ounces without the urn.*

What do you have when a group of conductors are up to their necks in wet concrete?
— *Not enough concrete.*

What's brown and black and looks good on a conductor?
— *A Doberman.*

What are semi-conductors?
— *Part-time musicians.*

A conductor and a violist are standing in the middle of an open road. Which one do you run over first?
— *The conductor. Business before pleasure.*

Define 'Conductor'.
— *A person who is skilled in following large groups of people at one time.*

Give an example of a collective noun.
— *'A plague of conductors'.*

If you drop a conductor and a watermelon off a tall building, which will hit the pavement first?
— *Who cares?*

Did you hear about the planeload of conductors on the way to the 'Winnipeg New Music Festival'?
— *The good news: It crashed.*
— *The bad news: There were three empty seats on board.*

What is the difference between a conductor and a baby?
— *A baby sucks its fingers.*

Why is a conductor like a condom?
— *It's safer with one but more fun without.*

What is the difference between alto clef and Greek?

— *Some conductors know how to read Greek.*

What do you get when you throw a conductor off a tall building?

— *Applause.*

What should one do after running over a conductor?

— *Back up.*

A prominent member of the orchestra came back from rehearsal one evening to find a smoldering crater where his house used to be. He ran to the nearest police officer to find out what happened. "While you were out the conductor came to your house, killed your family and burned it down." In shock, the musician replied, "Really? The conductor came to my house?"

Another musician called the symphony office to talk to the conductor. The musician is told that the conductor has died. Upon hearing this the musician called the office repeatedly with the same request. After receiving 20 calls from the same person, the receptionist asked the musician why he keeps calling. He happily replied, "I just like to hear you say it."

This guy walks into a pet store and notices a big bird in a cage with a price tag marked $20,000. "Why is this bird so expensive?" he asks the pet store owner. The pet store owner explains that the bird can sing any Italian opera, on request, with perfect intonation.

Amazed, the guy walks further into the store and notices a bigger bird and cage marked at $40,000. "What does this bird do?" the guy asks. "He can sing any Italian, French, or German opera on request." The guy continues to walk through the store when he notices the biggest bird and cage he's ever seen. The price tag says $80,000. "Wow, what does this bird do?" The pet store owner answers, "Nothing, but the other two birds call him Maestro."

At the annual *Conductors Of The World* conference Theobold Bohm, Leonard Bernstein and Herbert von Karajan were sitting in the hotel lounge discussing over drinks exactly who the greatest conductor of all time is. "Gentlemen," exclaimed Bohm, "I am the GREATEST conductor the world has ever had the privilege of witnessing !" "Not so," said Lenny, "why, just yesterday after a fabulous rendering of Beethoven's *9th Symphony*, the Lord spoke to me and

declared my direction and interpretation to be the best in all of Creation!" Von Karajan leapt up from his chair and screamed, "LIAR ! I never said anything of the kind !!!"

In the Cuisine part of this convention was overheard a recipe for cooking Conductors. The ingredients are as follows:

1 Conductor or two assistant conductors (avoid conductors laureate—they're too old and tough)

2 large cloves of garlic
1 tub lard or vegetable shortening
1 keg cheap wine
2 lbs assorted vegetables
4 lbs tofu

Upon capture, remove the tail and horns. Carefully separate the large ego and refrigerate for the sauce. Discard any batons, scores, pencils etc. Clean the conductor as you would a squid. After removing the slime and the inner organs (mostly large intestines), tenderize it on a rock with a strong pounding motion. Marinate it in a bathtub using half a keg of cheap wine. (No point in wasting the good stuff.) Exception: conductors from France or Italy. Also, Canadian and German conductors tend to have a beery aroma. Use your own discretion when choosing how to marinate them. When sufficiently soaked, remove the outside clothing and rub the complete surface area with garlic. Apply *all* of the vegetable shortening over the whole body. Place in a pan with the vegtables surrounding it.

Cover and cook on high until lightly flamed. When done, invite all members of the orchestra over for dinner and serve with the remaining wine.

Sauce: Combine the ego, seasonings and lots of ketchup in a blender and purèe until liquified. Heat and serve. Bon Appetit!

Found on the photocopier—the last page of 'Management Survey'

"... for considerable periods the three oboes have nothing to do. Their number should be reduced to one (1) and the work spread more evenly over the whole of the concert, thus eliminating excess activity.

"All twelve (12) first violins were playing identical notes. This is unnecessary duplication. The staff of this section should be reduced to four (4). If a larger volume of sound is required, it may be obtained by means of electronic amplifier apparatus.

"An increase in flute players is highly recommended pending budget approval. This conclusion was reached after one concert where the flutist was hardly heard at all. Having learned that flutes do not respond well to electronic amplifier apparatus, we are recommending an increase in the flute section from one (1) player to four (4).

"Much effort was absorbed in the playing of 16th notes. This seems to be an excessive refinement. It is recommended that all notes be rounded up to the nearest quarter note. If this were done, it would be possible to use trainees and lower-grade operatives more extensively. There seems to be too much repetition of some musical passages. Scores should be drastically pruned. No useful purpose is served by repeating on the horns a passage which has already been played on the strings. It is estimated that if all redundant passages were eliminated, the whole concert time of two hours could be reduced to 20 minutes, effectively cancelling the intermission.

"The conductor agrees generally with these recommendations, but expresses the opinion that there might be some falling off in attendance. In that unlikely event it should be possible to close sections of the auditorium entirely, with a consequent saving of overhead expence, lighting, salaries, for ushers, etc."

Vocals

Whether it be sopranos or baritones, the vocalist gets most of the venom in this book. When we metioned dirty jokes, this is the most likely place they would turn up. True to our word, the following anecdotes are pretty tame. There are some dirty ones here but they are the ones you probably won't get unless you are cursed with this particular profession.

This section is loosely divided into a few sections,—the SATB vocalists and the chorus singer (NOT 'chorus girl' jokes, as you all suspected).

Sopranos

Two fleas were talking about their travels one day. "I went to the symphony last night. I hitched a ride in the conductor's beard and stayed there for awhile. Things were great until the end of the first movement when I fell out and landed in the soprano soloist's cleavage. That was okay, nice and warm and all, but in the third movement she got all worked up and started to sweat. I ended up sliding down between her legs. I decided to just stay put and have a nap. What I don't get is when I woke up I was in the conductor's beard again."

Why can't a soprano drive faster than 68 kilometres per hour?
— *Because at 69 she blows a rod.*

What is the difference between a soprano and a terrorist?
— *You can negotiate with a terrorist.*

What is the difference between a soprano and a Porsche?
— *Most musicians have never been in a Porsche.*

What is the difference between a soprano and a pit bull?
— *The jewelry.*

What is the difference between a soprano and a pirhana?
— *The lipstick.*

How do you confuse a soprano?
— *Ask her to read the music.*

How many sopranoes does it take to change a lightbulb?
— *None. She thinks it's the accompanist's job.*

How many mezzo-sopranos does it take to change a lightbulb?
— *Who cares?*

How many sopranos does it take to change a lightbulb?
— *One. She holds it and the world revolves around her.*

Coloratura Soprano

How many coloratura sopranos does it take to change a lightbulb?
— *None. Her agent does that.*

Alto

What is the difference between a dressmaker and an alto?
— *A dressmaker tucks up the frills.*

How many altos does it take to change a lightbulb?
— *None, because they cannot reach that high.*

Why couldn't the alto perform for the conductor at her audition?

— *Because she forgot her diaphragm.*

How do you get an alto into a compact car?

— *Grease her hips and leave a donut on the dashboard.*

What is the definition of an alto?

— *A soprano who can sightread.*

What is the difference between an alto and a tenor?

— *The tenor doesn't have hair on his back.*

What is the difference between an alto and a toilet?

— *Toilets don't follow you around after you use them.*

How many altos does it take to screw in a lightbulb?

— *Two. One to screw it in and the other to say, "Isn't that a little high for you?"*

How do you put a twinkle in an alto's eye?
— *Shine a flashlight in her ear.*

Tenor

If you had all the tenors in the world laid end to end, what would happen?
— *The tenor population would be a much happier group of people.*

How many tenors does it take to change a lightbulb?
— *Three. One to do it, and two to bitch about how they could have done it if they had the high notes.*

How many counter-tenors does it take to change a lightbulb?

— *Two. One to buy the designer bulb and the other to say (slightly effeminately), "Fabulous!"*

What is the definition of a tenor?
— *Two hours before a nooner.*

How can you tell if a tenor is dead?
— *The wine bottle is still full and the comics haven't been read yet.*

Where is a tenor's resonance?
— *Where his brain ought to be.*

Define 'male quartet'.
— *Three men and a tenor.*

At a rehearsal for an opera, a tenor saw his arch-rival chatting with the conductor. Thinking that he might lose his spot, he demanded, "What are you doing?" The other replied, "Well next month I'm doing *Cosi* in Toronto and *Fidelio* in Montreal and..."

What is the difference between a soprono and a tenor?
— *About 10 kilograms.*

Baritone & Bass

What do you call 10 baritones at the bottom of the ocean?
— *A good start.*

When does a baritone sound his best?
— *When the tune is over.*

Define Aria.
— *The square footage taken up by a bassist's girth.*

What is the definition of an operatic 6/9 chord?
— *The augmented root of the bass is in the soprano.*

Chorus Singers

Why do high school choruses travel so often?
— *It keeps assassins busy.*

How does a young man become a member of a high school chorus?
— *On the first day of school he enters the wrong classroom.*

Popular Music

Much has been said about the place Pop Music has in our culture. Our friends in Europe have reluctantly embraced it, while our neighbours south of us here in the Great White North cannot get enough of the stuff. Whether you love it or hate it, Pop Music is here to stay.

I hope we don't upset anybody, but Rock, Jazz and Country are in this chapter together. Sorry, but that's just the way it is.

Drums

How do you get a drummer to play softer?
— *Put a sheet of music in front of him.*

What can you tell about a drummer who is drooling out of both sides of his mouth?
— *The stage is level.*

How can you tell when there is a drummer at your front door?
— *The knocking gets faster.* (See Percussion)

What does a dyslexic drummer do after a joke?
— *"Ching, ba-dum-dum"*

In what way are drum machines better than drummers?

— *Because machines keep a steady beat and won't sleep with your girlfriend.*

What do you call a girl who hangs out with musicians?

— *A Groupie* (See next joke).

What do you call a guy who hangs out with musicians?

— *A drummer.*

How many drummers from the Sixties does it take to change a lightbulb?

— *Ten. One to hold the bulb, and nine to drink until the room spins.*

What is the difference between a drummer and a drum machine?

— *You only have to punch the information into the drum machine once.*

How many drummers from the Seventies does it take to change a lightbulb?

— *None. Nothing really important happened in the Seventies anyway.*

How do you know when a drum solo is really bad?

— *Even the bass section notices.*

How many drummers from the Eighties does it take to change a lightbulb?

— *None. They have a machine that does that now.*

Two women were walking down the street when they heard a voice say "Hey, down here." They bent down and saw a talking frog. "If one of you kisses me, I will transform into a famous drummer and I will do anything for you!" One of the women reached down, scooped up the frog and slipped him into her pocket. "Why did you do that?" said one of them. Her friend replied, "I'm not an idiot. Everybody knows that a talking frog is worth more than a famous drummer!

How many drummers from the Nineties does it take to change a lightbulb?

— *Only one, but he will break 10 bulbs before realizing that they cannot just be pushed in.*

Why are bad drummers better than drum machines?

— *You don't have to plug them in to get something stiff, mechanical and uninspiring.*

Define 'musical oxymoron.'
— *Drum kit music.*

What is the last thing a drummer says to his band?
— *"Hey guys, how 'bout we try one of my songs?"*

Did you hear the one about the drummer who graduated from high school?
— *No, neither did I.*

Why is a drum solo like a sneeze?
— *You know it's coming but you can't stop it.*

How can you tell when a drummer is walking behind you?
— *You can hear his knuckles rasping on the ground.*

I asked my drummer to spell Mississippi. He asked me whether I meant the river or the state.

Guitar

How many lead guitarists does it take to change a lightbulb?
— *None. He gets the drummer to do it.*

How do you get a guitar player to play softer?
— *Give him a sheet of music.*

What is the best thing to play on a guitar?
— *Solitaire*

What do you call two guitarists playing in unison?
— *Counterpoint.*

How many guitarists does it take to change a lightbulb?
— *Three. One to do it and two to criticize his technique.*

How do you make a guitar player stop playing?
— *Put notes on the sheet of music.*

How many guitar duos does it take to screw in a lightbulb?

— *Only one, but they stand so close you'd swear that they were going to start necking.*

What would a rock guitarist do if he won a million dollars?

— *Keep playing until the gigs ran out.*

What did the guitarist say at his first gig?

— *Would you like fries with that?*

What do a vacuum cleaner and an electric guitar have in common?

— *Both suck when you plug them in.*

How do you get your mom to drive really fast?

— *Put your guitar in the middle of the road.*

Electric Bass

How many electric bass players does it take to change a lightbulb?

— *Four. One to change it and three to hold back the lead guitarist who is hogging the light.*

How do you get a bass player off your doorstep?
— *Pay for the pizza.*

How many bass players does it take to change a lightbulb?
— *None. The piano player can do it with his left hand.*

A man gives his son an electric bass for his 15th birthday, along with a coupon for four bass lessons. When the son returns from his first lesson, the father asks, "So, what did you learn?" "Well, I learned the first five notes on the E string." Next week, after the second lesson, the father again asks about the progress, and the son replies, "This time I learned the first five notes on the A string." Again one week later, the son comes home far later that expected, smelling of cigarettes and beer. So the father asks: "Hey, what happened in today's lesson?" "Dad, I'm sorry I couldn't make it to my lesson; I had a gig!"

Why don't bass players catch cold?
— *Even viruses have their pride.*

What did the bass player do when told to turn on his amp?
— *He caressed it softly and told it that he loved it.*

Heavy Metal

What is the most frequent heavy metal lie?
— *I AM NOT TOO LOUD!*

Punk Rock

How many punk rockers does it take to change a lightbulb?
— *Two. One to screw it in and the other to smash the old one on his forehead.*

Why can't punk rockers play reed instruments?
— *Ever try playing sax with a pierced?*

Singers

Pop Singers

How do you keep a singer in suspense?
— *Are you still waiting for the answer?*

Why does a rock star have to be up by six-thirty?
— *Most stores close by seven o'clock.*

One night, a lounge piano player pulls over the singer and says, "Now tonight we'll try a special version of this song: after five and a half measures of intro you come in with the second verse a minor third up, go to the bridge after 11 bars, twice moulate a half step down and halfway in the last A-section you start the tag, but a tritone lower. Are you ready? One, two,..." "Wait" the singer interrupts. "I'll never be able to do this!" The pianist replies, "But you nailed it last night!"

How do rock singers change a lightbulb?
— *They have a roadie set up the ladder and hand him the bulb.*

How do you know when there's a female vocalist at the door?
— *She can't find the key and doesn't know when to come in.*

How do you know that it's the lead singer knocking at your front door?
— *You open the door and she still doesn't know when to come in.*

What do you call a pop singer without a 'significant other'?
— *Homeless.*

What does a girl band vocalist's mother say to her before she goes out?

— *If you're not in bed by midnight you have to come home.*

Jazz Singers

How does a jazz singer make a million dollars?

— *He starts with two million.*

A doctor tells a jazz singer that he has cancer and only has a year to live. The jazz singer says, "What am I going to live on for a whole year?!!"

Country Singers

What happens when you spin a country singer's record backwards?

— *He gets his wife, his job and his John Deere back.*

Miscellaneous

This is the section that we just plopped everything else into. The reasons are easy to see. Everything from Bagpipes to New Age music, they're all here. Many of you purists out there are probably thinking, 'Wait a minute, accordions are keyboard instruments.' You can all go stand in the corner and think about what you just said.

Please keep in mind, we are not responsible for your inner child.

Accordion

What is an accordion good for?
— *An introductory course on map folding.*

What is a bassoon good for?
— *Kindling for an accordion fire.*

What is the difference between a lawnmower and an accordion?
— *You could sell a used lawnmower.*

Bagpipes

Why do bagpipers walk when they play?
— *To get away from the sound.*

What is the definition of a gentleman musician?
— *Someone who knows how to play the bagpipes but doesn't.*

What do you do when all the bagpipers in the world line up end to end to the moon and back?
— *Leave them there.*

What phrase do pipers never say?
— *Laddie, d'ya know what key we're in?*

What is the difference between a bagpipe and a chainsaw?
— *The chainsaw has greater dynamic range.*

How can you tell if a bagpipe is out of tune?
— *Because someone is playing it.*

Did you hear the one about the drummer who left his keys in the car at the gig?
— *It took him two hours to get the bagpiper out.*

Why don't Highland bagpipers have zippers on their kilts?
— *It might scare away the sheep.*

Why do pipers like to march when they play?
— *Because it's harder to hit a moving target.*

Why are the Irish still laughing at the Scots?
— *Because the Irish gave the Scots the bagpipe as a joke and the Scots still don't get it.*

How can you tell one pipe tune from another?
— *By the titles.*

What's the difference between a lawnmower and bagpipes?
— *You can tune a lawnmower and the owner's neighbours get upset if you borrow the mower without returning it.*

Ballet

A well-known ballet company recently did a cross-country tour. The tour started in Victoria, B.C., and ended in St.John's, Nfld. In each new city the company would perform with the local orchestra. On the first night, the bass trombone player approached the prima ballerina hoping she would go out with him. "Certainly not," said the prim young lady, "what would people think?" Not to be outdone, the bass trombone player exclaimed, "Well, all I was thinking about was dinner, there's no need to be snooty!" The very next day, however, she felt guilty and decided that he probably didn't mean any harm and promptly asked him out. He took her to dinner, and to her amazement she found herself having so good a time that she agreed to go back to his place for drinks. The next day she thanked him for a nice time and left with the company for the next city. Coincidentally, the very same thing happened in the next city with that orchestra's bass trombone player. In each city that she went to, the prima ballerina just happened to bump into these bass trombone players. In St. John's, the final stop of the tour, the same thing happened. "You trombone players are all such nice guys. Yes, I'd be happy to go out with you." Just as she touched his elbow, the bass trombone player's music folder fell open. On the bottom of the folder she read, 'For a hot time, see the prima ballerina!'

Banjo

Heard in a crowded shopping mall from a female five-string banjo player to her boyfriend: "Don't forget, honey, I need a new G-string."

What is the difference between a banjo and an anchor?

— *You tie an anchor to a rope before you throw it overboard.*

What is the least heard sentence among working musicians?

— *"Get a load of that banjo player's Porsche."*

What is the only thing that sounds worse than a banjo?

— *The sound of a chicken caught in a vacuum cleaner.*

What's wrong with a banjo player up to his neck in sand?

— *There isn't enough sand.*

Why did the banjo player marry the accordian player?

— *Upward mobility.*

What are you most likely to hear upon seeing a banjo player in a three-piece suit?

— *"Will the defendant please rise."*

What compliments a banjo the best?
— *A hack saw.*

Why is the banjo player a fiddle player's best friend?

— *Because without him, the fiddle player would be the most disliked person on Earth.*

Blues

How many blues players does it take to change a lightbulb?
— *None. They're all too laid back for that.*

One day, Robert asked his son Bob Jr, what he wanted to be when he grew up. "When I grow up I want to be a blues musician, Dad!" Robert replied, "You can't have it both ways, son."

Composers

Composers are bad pianists with good memories.

Why was the composer drunk?
— *Because he tried to use a tonic with his fifth.*

Why couldn't Mozart find his teacher?
— *Because he was Haydn.*

What do all the great composers have in common?
— *They are all dead.*

How can you tell if a composer is dead?

— *Hold out a cheque. Don't be fooled, though. He might still make a grasping action until his body stiffens completely.*

Knock, knock.
Who's there?
Knock, knock.
Who's there?
Knock, knock.
Who's there?
Knock, knock.
Who's there?
— *Philip Glass*

What did the gravedigger find when he dug up Beethoven's grave?

— *He was decomposing.*

What is the most common musical interpretation for an augmented fifth?

— *A 38-ounce bottle.*

Why did Mozart kill his chickens?

— *Because they always ran around going "Bach! Bach! Bach!"*

Folk Music

What is the difference between a violin and a fiddle?
— *Nobody minds if you spill beer on a fiddle.*

What is the definition of an optimist?
— *A folksinger with a mortgage.*

What is the difference between a folksinger and a puppy?
— *Eventually the puppy stops whining.*

Military Music

What do you get when you run an army officer over with a steamroller?
— *A-flat major.*

Why does an Air Force drummer have a half-ounce more brains than the captain's horse?
— *So he doesn't disgrace himself on parade.*

What do you get when you cross an Army Band French horn player and a goalpost?
— *A goalpost that can't march.*

Overheard during a routine band rehearsal, "Everybody go back to bar 108 and we'll start there," said the Navy Band director. One lost musician looked down on his music and said, "Where is that, Sir? Only bar 109 is marked!"

What is the definition of a relative major?
— *An uncle in a Guard's Band.*

Media

How many soundmen does it take to change a lightbulb?
— *None. "Hey man, I just do sound." or*
— *One, two, three. . . one, two, three.*

Did you hear about the new radio station CPMS?
— *They play three weeks of blues and one week of ragtime.*

Music Students

How many music students does it take to change a lightbulb?
— *One, but she gets two credits*

How many graduate music students does it take to change a lightbulb?

— *One, but the written thesis will take 10 years.*

Producers & Engineers

What are engineers tired of hearing at recording sessions?

— *"Turn it down? But I already turned it down..."*

How many producers does it take to change a lightbulb?

— *Hmm...I'm not sure...what do you think?*

One day, the musicians for a large recording session were assembling at a studio. Everyone had their headphones on and the session was about to begin when the producer said, "Okay, I need total silence." Just as he finished his sentence, the drummer played a big 'ba-dum, crash'. Furious, the producer screamed "Okay, who did that?"

New Age Music

What do you get when you play a new age song backwards?

— *Another new age song.*

About the Author

Daniel Theaker received his batchelor of music in flute and composistion at Mount Alison University. He is an Ottawa-based composer and flutist and has written 10 scale books for woodwinds and brass. His compositions include a set of *Three Preludes for Piano,* and three flute quartets that he recorded with his group, The Magellan Flute Quartet. He plays in the regimental band of the Governor General's Foot Guards. He lives with his friend Jen and his dog Saffie. He can be reached on his home page at: http://www.cyberus.ca/~daniel/

About the Cartoonist

Mike Freen has been doodling for as long as he can remember. He completed the cartoons for this book in 1997 at the age of 14. He comfortably resides in Kanata, Ont., with his family and his doodles.

Jacket design by Jim Stubbington.

A Working Musician's Joke Book

© Daniel G. Theaker, 1997
© Mike Freen (cartoons), 1997

All rights reserved

First published in Canada by
SOUND AND VISION
359 Riverdale Avenue
Toronto, Canada, M4J 1A4
www.soundandvision.com

First printing, August 1997

Canadian Cataloguing in Publication Data

Theaker, Daniel G. (Daniel George), 1967-
A working musician's joke book
isbn 0-920151-23-X
1. Music - Humor. I. Freen, Mike, 1983-
II. Title.
ML65.T374 1997   780'.207   C97-931528-X

Typset in Lucida Bright
Printed and bound in Canada